C000215645

LANDMARK COLLECTOR'S LIBRARY

The Spirit of
ASHBOURNE:2

Lindsey Porter

LANDMARK COLLECTOR'S LIBRARY

THE SPIRIT OF
ASHBOURNE:2
THE 20TH CENTURY IN PHOTOGRAPHS

Lindsey Porter

Landmark Publishing

Published by

LANDMARK
Publishing Ltd

Ashbourne Hall, Cokayne Ave
Ashbourne, Derbyshire DE6 1EJ England
Tel: (01335) 347349 Fax: (01335) 347303
e-mail: landmark@clara.net
web site: www.landmarkpublishing.co.uk

1st edition

ISBN 1 84306 065 5

British Library Cataloguing in Publication Data: a catalogue
record for this book is available from the British Library.

Printed by Bookcraft, Bath

Design & reproduction by James Allsopp

Cover captions:

Front cover: Union Street from the Market Place
Back cover top: Cottages, Dovehouse Green
Back cover middle: View from house in St John Street, 1904
Back cover bottom: Opening day, 1925, Mayfield Co-op

Page 1: Seven Arches, demolished in 1981
Page 2: Foster's Fishing Tackle shop, Church Street
Page 3: Green Man Yard with bay window, now removed

Contents

Back Bridge (with Dennis Walker & Sid, taken c. 1953)

Acknowledgements

I wish to thank the following for their assistance in the production of this book:

David Allsopp, Ashbourne News Telegraph, Mr A Avery, Janet Bayliss, Maisie Brown, David Burford, John Chadwick, Rob Dawson, M Evans, The late J Fleming, Mr Goddard, Mr C Gregory, Adrian Henstock, Cliff & Sandra Lewer, Sara Maslauskas, Peter Mellor, Julie Peake, J Pilkington, Teresa O'Ryan, George & Trilby Shaw, C Shemilt, Mrs Stone, Bill & Mary Stretton, Mark Titterton, Dennis Walker, Mary Winstone

Photographs marked English Heritage, NMR are Crown Copyright. Copies of these may be ordered from the National Monuments Record Centre, Kemble Rd, Gt Western Village, Swindon, SN2 2GZ, quoting the number given by the photograph (or the name in one instance).

INTRODUCTION

The Spirit of Ashbourne published to commemorate the Millennium has subsequently developed into a growing series of books, with 14 already published, and as many again in hand. Since the publication of Spirit of Ashbourne, a large number of photographs have been located which has enabled us to publish an additional volume. A particular feature is the number of street scenes, photographs of properties etc which should, I hope, jog a lot of memories. Certainly the series as a whole is doing just that!

Within Ashbourne it is surprising how much has changed in the last 50 years. Indeed, even excluding the large housing development close to the bypass, there seems to be a continual process of redevelopment. At the time of going to press, builders are working at the Grammar School in Green Road; on the Bath House site in Park Road; and on the new Sports & Community Hall project next to the swimming pool. Shortly we will see the redevelopment of the Dawson, Macdonald & Dawson site in Compton, plus the Queen Elizabeth's Grammar School Lower Site off Derby Road.

All this change creates a pressure on our town planners to preserve the essential fabric and character of the town. The subtlety of change reflected here in the change of occupations etc is one thing, but why was it necessary for us to lose the Bath House; the essential terraced character of Compton with the two Sainsbury's entrances; or to see the monstrous concrete structure built at the rear of the old Grammar School in Church Street? This book shows that the loss of the river running through Shaw Croft was the only remedy to serious flooding. However, the opportunity exists for a riverside walk as far as the bypass. Here is one development which could be a distinct improvement for locals and visitors alike; we need to look forward as well as back, drawing on the best of past experience.

I have found the production of this book full of surprises. I hope that my aspirations for it bring pleasant reading and happy memories of Ashbourne for you too.

Lindsey Porter   August 2002

The River Henmore at Dig Street, before the culvert was built. Photograph taken in 1959

Above: Taken in 1967 a good view of the former river bed in Dig Street. Having flowed down the northern edge of Shaw Croft, it turned through 90° to reach Compton Bridge

Right: Kenning's Garage and Langley House School behind it. Note the rooftop railings surrounding the school "playground"

Above: A familiar landmark demolished in the 1990s was the roadside house at Nestlé. The road has been realigned since this photograph was taken. The white gates were on the drive to Lodge Farm

Below: The aerodrome in 1971 with what looks like the beginning of the industrial development which has been successfully located on this site

Opposite page: School Lane showing the pre 1890 railway station. When the new station was built a footbridge over the railway line was also constructed. The lower view shows a similar scene, but note a footpath and a wall have been built along the boundary with the Paddock

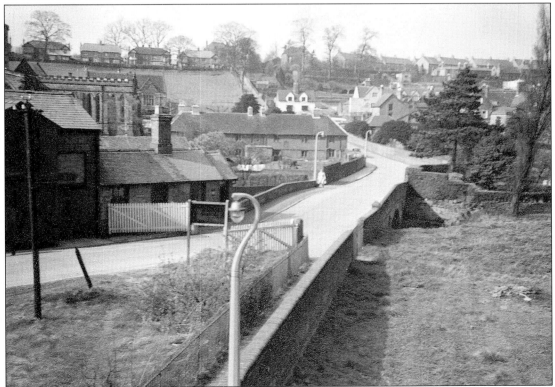

Two views of Station Street – Station Road area. Both were taken after 1901, when the Station Hotel opened. The new railway station is on the left. The upper photograph is the older of the two; the last section of Station Street still remaining undeveloped

A well-loaded steam wagon pauses outside the Station Hotel (now Beresford Arms Hotel), opposite the Railway Station. Note the railings around the trees and Bank Croft

A delightful view of Seven Arches railway bridge, just north of the tunnel. See also p. 1 for a view of the path under the arches

A goods train heading for Clifton from Ashbourne

A lovely view of the Primitive Methodist Chapel in Station Street, now replaced by a terraced row of houses. The chapel opened in 1895 at a cost of £1,465 and seated 120 people

Right & Below: Chaos in St John Street when the road was completely replaced in 1961. Note Bagnalls & Howell & Marsden on the right

Below: A wonderful view of St John Street in 1904. Horses, carts and carriages fill the street before the conflict of cars, lorries and pedestrians. Despite the obvious need today for a bypass, the provision of such a route seems as far away as ever. Unfortunately, lip-service from politicians provides us with no solution at all to pedestrian safety

A view to St John Street in 1966

At least Victoria Square, formerly Butchers Row/The Shambles is now virtually traffic free. The area has seen some changes over the years. Notice the Leek United & Midlands Building Society building and its predecessor; the presence of Melias next to The Horns and the inn sign of The Tiger Inn, now the Lamplight Restaurant

The last day of service at the railway station. The engine driver and his fireman posed for photographs along with civic leaders (see also p16). The station closed on 1st June, 1964. The site was redeveloped as the swimming pool and adjacent car park. Albert Dawson is on the far left

Two more views (above) of the last day of steam and also the last showing at the Empire Cinema (right), on the site of the Empire Social Club. The cinema opened on 3rd June, 1912, a week late following an electrical problem on the original opening night of the previous week

Advertising hoardings in 1951 facing Station Road, next to the railway station

A similar view, looking across the road. The signal box on the right also features above

A wintery scene looking towards the Goods Yard and Nestlé from alongside the River Henmore

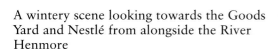

HOUSES & YARDS

2

Above: A view in olden times of cottages on Dovehouse Green at the junction with North Avenue and Northcliffe. The basic structure of these properties was retained when they were redeveloped although they now have a different front elevation

Below: Union Street in 1961

Above: A close up of the top buildings seen in the bottom scene of p18, taken on the same day

Middle: Another view of Union Street, this time looking towards Dovehouse Green. The end block of buildings in the last photograph appear as the middle group in this scene

Below: The rear of some three-storey buildings in Union Street

Three more views of the rear of property in Union Street, all derelict and awaiting demolition

Houses off the Market Place and the Channel, including Slater's shop on the left,
which stood on the corner of Union Street

Above: Tiger Yard, off The Market Place

Below: Smiths Yard, Church Street

Above: Wells Yard which was situated behind Howell & Marsden's shop,
now Bookthrift & Pretty Polly, with one of the residents hanging out her washing

Below: Salt Alley Yard, showing the row of houses that stretched down to the river

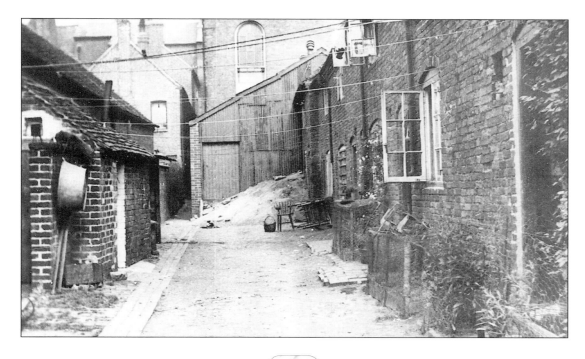

Above: Taken in 1949, the two houses and shop which stood on the site of what was Sheila Spencer's clothing shop, now the White Peak Dental Practice, Compton. To the left is Malbon's Yard. The shop bears a sign saying 'Ward' and aspidestras fill the downstairs windows of the two houses. English Heritage, NMR; AA50/2686

Below left: The former shop and house that stood at the Compton end of Cooper's Yard (next to Benny's Pizza House) now the entrance to Sainsbury's Supermarket

Below right: The above property and adjacent house from Cooper's Yard

Above: Malbon's Yard, on the west side of Compton, looking west

Below: Another view of Malbon's Yard, looking east towards
Compton, note the barrels for collecting water

Above: The Stag & Pheasant Yard behind the inn of that name on the east side of Compton

Below: The Terrace showing the end of Compton Bridge. These properties are on the site of the Health Centre. A gate on the left (not visible) gave access to Shaw Croft (see p. 154) and there was also a slope down to the river – possibly a relic of the days when there was a tannery in Compton

Two additional views of The Terrace showing (above) the view to the river (not visible) and (below) the shop on the right abutting Chapel Yard. There were further properties behind The Terrace and some of these are shown on page 30

Above: Chapel Yard, looking towards Compton and showing (on the left) the property, behind the shop in the last photograph (p. 27)

Two more views (middle and bottom) showing the four two-storey houses on the north side of Chapel Yard

Above: Former houses on the west side of Old Hill

Left: Houses in 1960 on the junction of Station Street and Station Road. The taller one on the right still survives

Below: Building work commences in 1977 in the grounds of The Firs, at the bottom of Derby Road

Above: A view taken in 1904 consisting of three photographs put together. The garden on the left belongs to Madge House, St John Street and the view is towards The Park and Shaw Croft, with Sandy Lane, now Park Road, running across the middle. The curved line from Sandy Lane across The Park marks a footpath. This remarkable scene shows how rural much of Ashbourne was until the 1920s, especially as The Paddock existed beyond Compton and it originally extended to eight acres. The houses (right) are in Salt Alley Yard

Below: Behind the Terrace in Compton was a small row of houses facing Shaw Croft. Here is a view of them just prior to demolition. There is another view of these cottages on page 84 of Spirit of Ashbourne Volume 1. There was another row behind and parallel to The Terrace too

Above: Ashbourne Hall from Spalden Avenue, 1921, showing the Council development in progress. The Hall displays its 1850s extension to the rear of the Georgian house, lacking character and looking more like a factory development

Below: The laying out of Cokayne Avenue and The Park in c. 1920. The alder trees which line the grass verges have just been planted. The site of the Park estate may clearly be seen

Three views of Ashbourne Hall in 1949

Above: The main front door; the right hand side was in use as offices

Right: The bay (now demolished) appears to be the entrance for a vehicle. The top floor of the left side of the house was removed within a few years of this being taken. The first floor retains no architectural features; a pity as the main room at the front was "The Lady's Bedroom". "The Master's Bedroom" was above the right hand bay (and presumably was the room occupied by Bonnie Prince Charlie)

Left: The West Front. Much of this was sold in small units. Eventually the left half of six bays plus the top floor of the right half were removed. What is left awaits a "make-over" of paint to match the remaining three-storey portion. It currently looks badly in need of it. All English Heritage, NMR; AA50/2666, 2665, 2664

Two views of the Alrewas Mill Cottages formerly sited adjacent to Bond's Mill and the River Dove. There were seven in a row, plus two more, slightly downstream from the rest

Above: Cottages known as The Rock Houses situated at the roadside
on Bridge Hill, Mayfield, all now demolished

Below: The cottage on the corner opposite the Queen's Arms,
which is still intact, although its fence has gone

Above: "Sunnyside", the Mayfield home of Mr Simpson, owner of Mayfield Mills. Like "The Firs" (see p29), the grounds have been developed for housing, now The Park

Below: Another elegant house is Mayfield House. Here is a view of it in c.1952 showing the east front

Birch Terrace, off Station Street

In the distance may be seen The Cottage Hospital, later converted into apartments, standing in front of a large house which has subsequently been demolished. Taken in 1905

A careful look at this scene reveals many of the yards and other properties which have now gone, including the Wesleyan Chapel which gave Chapel Yard off Compton (see p. 28) its name

Foster's Fishing Tackle shop. Here rods and artificial flies were manufactured to a high standard. This photograph, taken in 1949, shows the business in Church Street. English Heritage, NMR; AA50/2683

A lot of photographs of the Market Place show agricultural machinery in the area of The Vaults. These items belonged to W. Barnes, whose premises may be seen on this photograph, taken in 1962, together with several items for sale. Shopkeepers were quite content to extend out into the Market Place as the photograph below shows. Note Spencers Shop, now further up this side to the right. The two-storey properties were replaced in 1897

Produce scattered over the pavement was a feature of the Town Hall side of the Market Place too. The upper photograph is the oldest of the two shown. Kennedy's Ironmongers was next to the Town Hall; then came Charles Gregory's shop; another (not identified) and then J H Henstock's printing office. The lower view has not altered a lot except the shop of Sellers & Son showing a double-bay window. The gas lamps lended almost a touch of elegance. The Council has contemplated replacing the iron work around the Wright memorial. The upper scene shows how it should look

Above: Taken in 1949, this view shows J C Lee & Son occupying the bottom two properties of the Market Place, with Boots and Woolworths beyond in St John Street. Lee's described themselves as "Sight Testing Opticians". Note the Tudor Café sign; the café being above Lee's shop. Boots have a sign announcing that they have a "Farm and Gardening Department". English Heritage, NMR; AA50/2695

Below: This scene, from 1949, shows the properties above the Elite Cinema. From the left were Kennedy's Ironmongers, Bradley's Post Office, Hunters and then Kennedy's Cycle & Sports Dept. English Heritage, NMR; AA50/2260

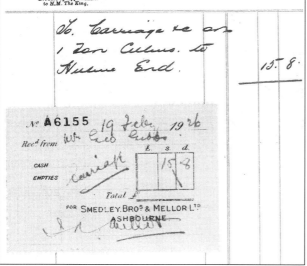

National Telephone No. 6.
Established over 60 Years.

MARKET PLACE,
ASHBOURNE, -6 FEB 1926 192

Mr *Geo Gibbs*

DR. TO

SMEDLEY BROS. & MELLOR, Ltd.,

WHOLESALE AND FAMILY

Grocers, Wine & Spirit Merchants,

PROVISION IMPORTERS.

Agents for Worthington & Co., Ltd.

Brewers by Appointment
to H.M. The King.

To. *Carriage &c on*
1 Ton Culms. to
Hulme End.

15. 8.

N^o A6155 19 *Feb.* 1926

Rec^d from *Mr Geo Gibbs*

	£	s.	d.
CASH	*carriage*	15	8
EMPTIES			
Total £			

FOR SMEDLEY BROS & MELLOR L^TD
ASHBOURNE

Above: Adjacent the Town Hall was Carter's Café and Bed & Breakfast. The café was open on a Sunday but Mr Jennings' cobblers shop is shut for the day. Taken in 1949. English Heritage, NMR; AA50/2697

Left: An invoice dated 1926 from Smedleys (see p. 42)

Above: Above Mr Jennings was Woodisse's, that wonderful old-fashioned ironmongers which, somewhere, had everything! To their left was Smedley Brothers & Mellor, agents for Worthington's Brewery – which meant brewer's grains as well as ale – as the invoice shows (see previous page). Again the photograph was taken on a Sunday in 1949. Woodisse's closed in 1977. English Heritage, NMR; AA50/2259

Below: Opposite the Elite Cinema, at Middle Cale, in 1949 stood this property occupied by Micki Johns Ltd, Electrical Engineers, at Electricity House with Wyles shoe shop above.

Despite the shops being shut, there appears to be a market with stalls attracting shoppers. Interesting, as this was probably taken on a Sunday. English Heritage, NMR; AA50/2694

Above: Above Electricity House was Wyles Brothers Ltd, a shoe shop which also faced the main part of the Market Place. The chip shop and British Legion look much the same today, but the gas lamp has gone. English Heritage, NMR; AA50/2256

Below: Next to the British Legion in 1949 were Cash & Co, another shoe shop, in premises now part of the British Legion. Next door in the double, square-bayed shop now occupied by the Tourist Information Centre, was Wibberley's general provisions. The White Swan was an Ind Coope house. English Heritage, NMR; AA50/2257

Baylis's wholesale confectioners, now part of the British Legion occupying the premises later taken over by Cash & Co (see previous page)

Above: Many older residents will remember Mr Shemilt's sweet shop and tobacconists on the corner of Buxton Road and King Street. Here it is in March 1950, advertising Wills Wood-bines, Player's Craven A and Capstan cigarettes. At this time, however, it was occupied by B A Stockton. For the view on the opposite side of the street, see p68.
English Heritage, NMR; AA50/2254

Below: The top of the Market Place in the 1940s. Slater's shop has been demolished on the Union Street corner and what became "Top Spencers" was the Bradley House Café with Spencer's Café adjacent. The cobbles have become the preserve of the motor car. The sooner this area is pedestrianised, the better!

Above: The staff at Spencers c. 1910, with William Spencer's sisters

Below: This remarkable traction engine and train of four waggons is believed to be heading for Ilam Hall, causing a diversion for shoppers

It is surprising how many people call this area The Butchery. It was Butchers Row until a century ago and probably never officially called The Butchery, but it is nice that the link is still maintained. A deed of 1874 also indicates that Butchers Row was then also known as The Shambles.

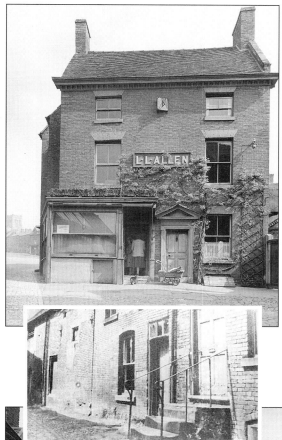

Left: Allen's shop is now the bookies, looking down towards St John Street, This view dates from 1949 and Allens may have been butchers as a sign reads 'Register here for meat, bacon, eggs'. Two ladies and perhaps the cat wait for post-war rations, while a baby sleeps in its push-chair. The bookies was then next to the White Swan. English Heritage, NMR; AA50/2252

Middle: The Gallery

Below: Victoria Square in 1949, looking towards Coates' shop and DeVilles the butchers, now Hollingsworths. Beyond is Gregorys, Howell & Marsden (advertising Benedict Peas & Bovril), William Deacons bank and across Dig Street, Hawksworth & Newbold who were adjacent to the Cock Inn. English Heritage; NMR; AA50/2249

The shop of Mr Osborne who started the Ashbourne News and rescued Jimmy Harrison from drowning in Clifton Mill Pond at Shrovetide, 1878. He had previously been shipwrecked off the Isle of Wight and swam ashore. The shop is now occupied by WH Smith. The bank is shown before the building was defaced by a modern front. It was formerly the Birmingham District & Counties Bank

The end of The Gallery divided either side of these premises into St John Street. The wooden shelter now occupies this site. On the extreme right is the Co-op. The demolished shop was a greengrocers. To the left was the Co-op bakery; a shop selling ? crockery etc and then there was Osborne & Beeby's chemist, now Bennetts

Above: The view into St John Street, early in the 20th century

Below: A close-up of the butcher's shop behind the Green Man sign.
Note also the original appearance of Blue's Hairdresser's in Victoria Square

This timber framed building probably survived for four centuries before being demolished in the first half of the 20th century. Note the barber's poles once a common feature in urban streets. The replacement building is occupied by Bookthrift

Above: This would appear to be the staff of Howell & Marsden, The company demolished the property shown on p49

Below: Despite displaying a sign for "Garage" and "Petrol", the town's streets were still dominated by the horse and cart rather than motor vehicles. This postcard is dated 1912. The buildings facing the camera on the left have been replaced. The sign reads: "Imperial Laundry, Beautiful Snow White Linen", but the shop was a butchers. F. Whilock kept the Refreshment Rooms

Above: St John Street in c.1910. Another barber's pole may be seen, plus the property on p48 and now demolished – removed to widen the pavement, no doubt, as it is rather narrow at that point

Below: Looking back towards Church Street in 1958. Not a lot has changed. Howell & Marsden are still there, but the Green Man sign has been replaced. English Heritage, NMR; St John St. Ashbourne

Above: A further view taken in 1977 towards Church Street, this time from Wigley's shoe shop. Dewhursts came to Ashbourne in the mid 1930s. Signs in the window show that turkey was 49p per lb; sirloin 96p and topside 99p per lb. To the right is Macs Army Store. The timber sticking out of the second floor window was to support the structure. You can see that it was also braced on the photograph below

Left: Just visible in the photograph above is this shop which was occupied by This 'n' That. The sign in the window announces that they were moving to The Gallery on 17th October (1977) prior to demolition of the building. English Heritage, NMR; BB77/10888

Above: Wigley's shoe shop, being boarded up ready for Shrovetide in 1957

Below: Mr H T Spencer, presumably with his son outside the Gingerbread Shop. The front has been significantly altered. See also p. 72

A view taken in 1949. It shows Smith's Wine House, now Smith's Tavern. Prior to this, it was Smith & Sons Wine Merchants. Their two square-bay windows were full of bottles of wine, beers and Guinness. It had a small counter where on-sales could be drunk and was occupied by Smith & Son in 1895. It became the Wine House between 1947-49, when it was a free house. This view also shows Burgons (grocers) and Fredwyns (hairdressers), followed by Boots and Woolworths. Dewhursts eventually moved into Burgons property. (see p52). English Heritage, NMR; AA50/2701

The frontage facing the former Co-op and before the wooden shelter was erected. Taken in 1970

Two views along the street before and after
the removal of the building shown on p47.
Woolworths closed in 1977, the same year as
Woodisse's (then known as Desborough &
Woodisse) in the Market Place

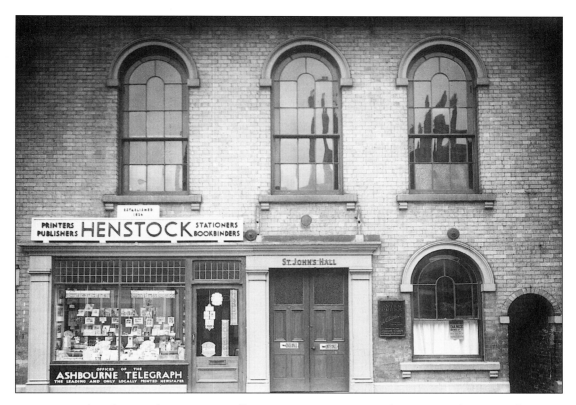

J H Henstock's shop and newspaper office in 1935, occupying what is now the Art Gallery in St John Street

The window appears to be displaying some of Dr Hollick's books on the North Staffordshire Railway and also one of his model locos. The books were presumably printed by Henstocks

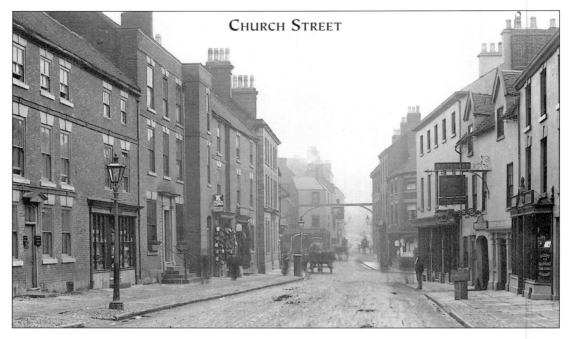

Above: Church Street, from one of R & R Bull's postcards dated 1904

Below: The Westminster Bank in 1950 adjacent to Bayliss Bros, tobacconists and newsagents. The Bank amalgamated with the National Provincial Bank in 1967. In the 1500s a wayside cross stood at this junction, the cast iron sign being its final successor. The postbox bears the monogram 'VR', but the box has not survived, at least not in Ashbourne. English Heritage, NMR; AA50/2677

Above: Boots the Chemist, also in 1949, prior to moving to St John Street. To the left is the baker's shop of C Richardson. The bakery was behind the shop and has now been converted to an attractive dwelling house. In between these shops was a ladies and gents hairdressers. In 1895, there were two bakeries in Church Street. English Heritage, NMR; AA50/2679

Hulme's Fish and Game shop in 1949, when its window only occupied the middle portion of the building. In 2001, Hulme's announced that because of petty regulations from Brussels, they were no longer able to dress and sell game after doing so for 70 years. English Heritage, NMR; AA50/2208

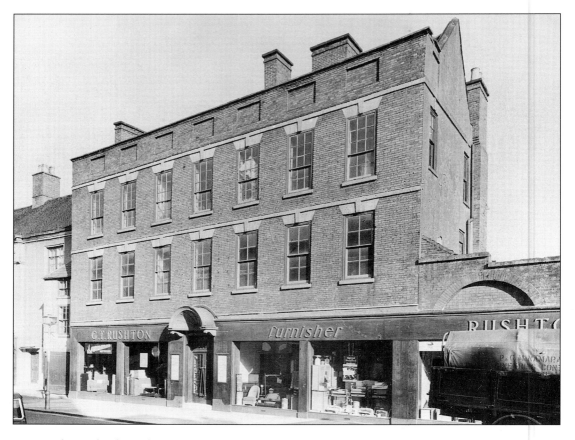

G T Rushton the furnishers, cabinet makers and upholsterers, next to Hulmes.
English Heritage, NMR; BB69/5778

Church Street decorated
with bunting. On the left
is the Savings Bank

The Savings Bank, (already the Trustee Savings Bank according to a sign in the window), which closed in 2001, after merging with Lloyds Bank. This view dates from 1949 and shows how elegant the frontage is. English Heritage, NMR; AA50/2186

Left: The former bakery and shop in King Street (the three-storey property)

The former Staffordshire Farmers' premises in Park Road. Recently occupied by Ashbourne Taxis (bottom photograph) along with the Bath House (middle), both of which were demolished in 2002. One used the Bath House if you did not have a bath at home. It was built in the 1860s

Dig Street in 1949, with RW (Reggie) Bayliss's confectioners;
then Parwich Dairy and J M Callow. English Heritage, NMR; AA50/2248

Above: The view down Dig Street in 1959 towards the advertising
hoardings on the bank of the River Henmore

Below: Hunter's Tea Stores in Dig Street, situated on the west side

Above: A Shrovetide photograph but included for the view it gives of Dig Street. Note the old Cock Inn on the right, at the end of the street on the site of the new shops. The position of Hunters, see previous page, may be clearly seen

Below: The interior of Sheila Spencer's Fashion House in Compton, now the Dental Practice

Above: May Taylor's Bakery in Station Street, opposite North Leys

Right: The grocers shop on the corner of Station Street and Station Road with Mrs Gee. Both of these photographs were taken c. 1960

Above: Slater's shop, Mayfield. In addition to being Grocers and Bakers they advertised Hackney Carriages for hire. The people are outside Radford's Shop, now demolished

Below: The former Co-op in Coneygreave Lane, Mayfield, in 1925 on the opening day. It is now boarded up

This section is by no means a complete selection of photographs of the town's inns and some, such as the Tiger, Durham Ox, Cross Keys and Roebuck, may be found *In and Around Ashbourne in Victorian Times*. See also p. 55 for Smith's Wine House.

Above: The White Lion Hotel on Buxton Road in 1949. It is now Bramhalls. The wedding scene in the above mentioned book on p198 was taken in the White Lion Yard. In this photograph, the landlord was Clarence Jones and the pub was called Alton's White Lion, Alton's were brewers of Derby. The property above the hotel, Carrington House, is also advertising accommodation. English Heritage, NMR; AA50/2689

The White Horse, situated just below The White Lion

Above: The Horns was a small three-roomed pub until Mr Hollingsworth closed his popular butchers shop. This was then added to the pub. Here it is seen when the shop was occupied by Gallimore's in 1949. In 1895, this pub was called the Stag Horns. English Heritage, NMR; AA50/2250

Below: The Green Man & Blacks Head Royal Hotel before the sign was renewed and when traffic flowed bothways along St John Street

Above:
A Shrovetide crowd outside The Coach & Horses Inn in Dig Street. The premises have subsequently been rebuilt

Left: The White Hart Yard before the building over the arch was removed

Above: The Machine Inn, next to the traffic lights in Sturston Road. It was named after an adjacent weighing machine. The pub and house could have had little or no rear yard, which may have been why they were demolished, see p. 145

Below: The Railway or The Railway Commercial & Family Hotel as it was earlier called. The premises survive in Station Street. See overleaf also. This photograph was taken in 1960

Above: This photograph turned out to be quite a surprise when it was identified. It shows the Ashbourne Gingerbread shop prior to the addition of the mock timber effect. Sowter's shop (behind the man) is now Natural Choice, but is unrecognisable as the front of the building has been replaced. Nearest the camera is the Horse & Jockey Inn. This closed in 1899. The key to the identification is the 3-storey building in the background and the faint pub sign

Right: The gable of The Railway had an advert which has been a remarkable survivor. This photograph was taken in 1996 and it had only started to deteriorate shortly prior to that

Above: The Beresford Arms Hotel, previously The Station Hotel, pictured from across the railway. It was originally a tied house for J Eadie's Brewery of Burton. If you look carefully at the two doorways, you can see the company's trade mark (a red cross) carved in the stone-work and featuring in the stained glass above the doors. It was opened in 1901 and this scene was taken sixty years later

Below: The Queen's Arms, Hanging Bridge, from Bridge Hill, Mayfield. This view also shows the building to the right of the road which had a variety of uses including a cheese factory and a builder's store

Above: The Royal Oak Hotel with a party of visitors when Agnes A Bassett was licensee

Below: The Duke of York Inn which gives its name to the petrol station on Mayfield Road

The Old Malthouse in Union Street, 1961. Ashbourne was a centre for production of malt and its ale was held in good regard. When the building was demolished, an underground passage was uncovered (below). It must have been used for cold storage of malt or ale

FLOODING

5

The loss of the River Henmore flowing through the town is still lamented on occasions. Here is a reminder of the floods which occurred when the river overflowed its banks. In fact most of the scenes show the last of the big floods, in 1965.

The river by Compton Bridge with water flooding cars parked behind the hoardings

Above: Compton under water with floods heading up towards the traffic lights. This view also shows Sheila Spencer's shop, Benny's Pizza House (the Old Durham Ox Inn) and the property now demolished by Cooper's Yard

Below: A policeman carries a grateful child across the street. Water can be seen lying in Cooper's Yard (top left)

Left: Water in Dig Street, where it often reached the traffic lights

Below: Kenning's Garage underwater (bottom) together with the area behind (middle)

Above: Shaw Croft looking like a lake. This was taken from Back Bridge

Below: Staffordshire Farmers' stores under several feet of water

Two views of Peter Street during the flood of 1963

Right: The fire station with more water than it needed

Below: The Fish Pond; at this size it could have been an attraction in itself if it wasn't so dangerous. The water stretches from the Park Estate, across to the river (see middle) and also covered the recreation ground

The answer was to culvert the river and here are two scenes
showing it under construction in 1970 at Shaw Croft

The opening of the bus station was covered in *Spirit of Ashbourne :1* p. 91. Here are views before and after construction of the shelter and in use with a double decker bus when opened in 1955

The old building adjacent to the toilet block was used as the fire station before moving to Park Road. It was probably the foundry building of James Bassett who cast the milestones on the road to Leek. Before that it was possibly the 18th century copper metal warehouse of J Ride & Son.

Above: This was taken to record a diversion of buses in 1957 but also shows the cottages now demolished (far left) and the former mill buildings (far distance)

Below: The new fire station in Park Road, having just been completed, in 1959

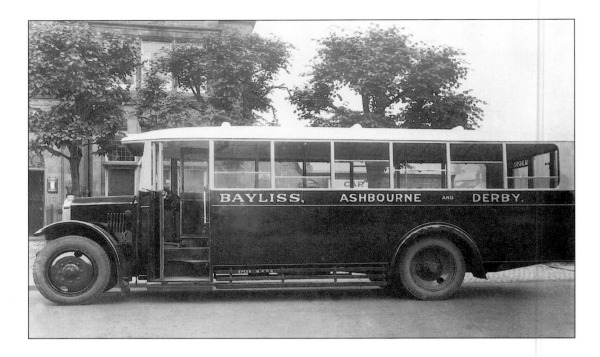

In *Spirit of Ashbourne: 1*, reference is made to Bayliss's buses based on material from the local paper (see p242). Janet Bayliss advises that this was not quite correct and has kindly supplied the following on Ashbourne's former local bus company:

"In the mid-twenties, a model T Ford bus was put into service between Ashbourne and Derby. The business quickly expanded until a fleet of 12 buses was operating by 1930. Competition with the Trent Company was extremely fierce. Speeding to reach stops first and pick up the passengers was widely practised. The police frowned on this and drivers were often summonsed. Mr. Albert Lawrence Bayliss was even summoned twice in one day. Although the competition was cut-throat, the return fare to Derby at one stage being only 10d, the business prospered until 1930. The government then introduced new laws setting up the Office of Traffic Commissioner to supervise bus services, timetables, fares etc., also to improve safety and prevent the sort of rivalry which led to risk taking and accidents. Mr Bayliss realised that the halcyon days were over and sold his business to the London, Midland & Scottish Railway Company who in turn disposed of it to the Trent Company. Some of the drivers and conductors took up employment with Trent." Here is a view of one of their buses outside the Station Hotel.

The removal of the tree lined path fronting St Oswald's Church in 1958 robbed the town of a valuable amenity. Here are some views of it. Bulmer's Directory of 1895 states "Along the north side [of the church] is a fine avenue of lime trees, stretching about a quarter of a mile, which is a favourite resort of the town's people and visitors."

Gates from Church Walk leading into Mayfield Road

AT WORK

8

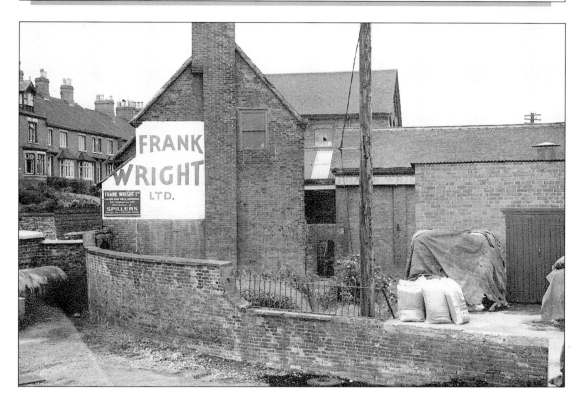

Above: Frank Wright's former mill premises on the Clifton Road corner of School Lane. The building may also be seen on the bottom left corner of the photograph on p9 (top)

Right: Between the buildings above and the old railway goods shed was a building which bears the sign 'JO Jones & Sons, Corn Mill'. Jones's also operated from Clifton and Okeover Mills

Above: Taken in 1977, an early view of the Industrial Estate and Blenheim Road where Messrs F Wright relocated

Below: Another firm to relocate there was Hill & Webster. This is their old premises at North Lees

Two views of the 1846 handpress on which the *Derbyshire Advertiser* was first printed. It was still in use from time to time by J H Henstock in St John Street in the 1930s. The lower view shows a poster for the sale of nearly 100 beasts at Shirley Common Farm in October 1933

Above: The staff of J H Henstock & Son Ltd at The Avian Press in 1929. Seated centre is Joseph H Henstock; on his left is Frederick Wm. Henstock (his brother). On his right is John H Henstock, his son, and standing, centre rear, is Laurence F Henstock, his nephew

Below: A poor quality photograph showing Joseph Harrison and his furniture removal wagons, hauled by a traction engine. He also had his own railway wagons. The scene is adjacent to Church Walk

The large building beyond the Union Street toilets must have abutted Slater's shop in the Market Place (see front cover). The building was used as Hunt's bakery and also by a tea merchant. It is believed that the town's horse-drawn fire engine was also kept here. Above the bakery was living accommodation. It would be interesting to know more of its early history; it looks more like a commercial building than anything else. It is understood that it was demolished in the 1930s

Another lost bakery is Bates's, which closed in 1999. Above is Brian Bates on Ash Wednesday, 1999 outside the bakery gates having turned up the Shrovetide ball. The other views show the bakery (left) following closure including the oven which had baked its last loaf. By the oven are Brian and David Bates (opposite)

After Bayliss's buses were sold off (see p. 86), their Compton premises were retained and A L Bayliss, son of H D Bayliss, opened a garage there. An engineering works developed there too. The premises were between David Neill Mica Hardware and H Smith's grocery shop. They eventually moved to the Industrial Estate, where they specialise in automatic greenhouse ventilation equipment

Above are the premises in 1936 and (left), the Bayliss Garage breakdown wagon in Station Road, c.1936. Behind the vehicle, the railway station passenger bridge is visible. The trees on the left are outside the Station Hotel.

Bayliss's Compton workshop in 1962 and the lubrication bay of the garage, taken in the 1930s

The original frontage of
Dawson, McDonald &
Dawson together with the
adjacent property removed
for Lumbard's Garage and (?)
formerly the Stag & Pheasant
Inn. The bottom photograph
was taken in 1964 and clearly
post-dates the other two. At
the time of going to press
(September 2002), this
property was emptied prior
to demolition

Above: Mayfield Mills, showing the houses by the River Dove and "Sunnyside", high on the hill. The mill was originally powered by the River Dove, using a water wheel, but steam power was eventually substituted, hence the chimney

Below: The steam engine, installed at Mayfield Mill. The photograph was taken by Mayfield photographer Mr Moscrop, who took many of the old postcard scenes around the village that survive to this day. By the engine is Mr Allen

Construction of the Nestlé works began with building the chimney from specially tapered bricks. Here it is finished, as the steel framing is constructed for the buildings. A flag flies at the top to mark its completion in 1910. Around the top of the chimney may be seen a row of white crosses, set against the red of the brickwork. Nestlé is a Swiss-owned company and the Swiss flag is a white cross on a red background!

Another view of the new chimney with the Clifton Road houses to the right

Construction of foundation work. Note the old house in the background

The buildings beginning to take shape

Four views of the factory under construction (this page and overleaf)

Installation of the
Babcock boilers prior to
building the boilerhouse

The boilerhouse and
adjacent buildings
nearing completion

The completed works (above) and a later view (below)

Recent "brown field" site developments in the town have been the single site extensions for Queen Elizabeth's Grammar School (this page), the demolition of the former cattle market and redevelopment with housing (p 110) and current development of the Bath House site (p 62) and of course the extension to the Sports Hall and Swimming Baths (p 116)

Here are four views of the new school buildings rising around
the current Green Road site, in Febuary, 2002

Three views of the
former cattle market
buildings, allbeit taken
after the cattle pens
(made of cast iron by
W Barnes & Co of the
Market Place) had
been removed from
beyond the large shed.
The stone-built
building near the top
of the site probably
dates back to the
opening of the market

Above: The right hand side of the large building shown on the previous page

Below: The site redeveloped by Birch plc with three and two-storey town houses

Above: Advertising hoardings on Mayfield Road

Below: A lovely view of a steam driven roller parked on Mayfield Road and ready for work. It is at the same location as the view above, where Dove Service Station is now situated

Three views of old buildings in the town being demolished. Top right: the old buildings on the site of the Compton Dental practice. The other two show the demolition of the Terrace (above) and Chapel Yard (below) in 1966

The northern end of Nestlé showing the buildings demolished a couple of years ago.
These two scenes were taken as milk churn deliveries terminated

Building the telephone exchange in Park Road in 1965 (above) and houses in Mayfield in 1900 (below). The latter is Oxmead Terrace adjacent to Mayfield Avenue and opposite the now boarded-up former Co-op (see p. 67)

The new Sports hall and Community Centre being constructed in July 2002.
The view is from School Lane bridge

As the century drew to a close, the corporate life of the town continued its work. Plans for a millennium clock came to fruition and councillors wrestled with thorny problems such as the one-site school and its funding (which involved redevelopment of the "lower site" off Derby Road) and the type of housing required on the old cattle market. The town's major requirement – a north-south bypass – remained as far away as ever. That, however, lacks funding at a county level and is out of the hands of the town's council. Here are a few scenes of activity in the year 1999-2000

Above: The Ashbourne Town Council, Year 1999-2000. Front Row (l-r): Fred Elliott; Ian Bates; Simon Spencer; Mayor Alan Hodkinson; Andrew Birch; Jenny & Vince Ferry. Back Row (l-r): Alan Lee, Ray Marrison, Tony Millward, John Hollingsworth, Mrs Pam Woodyatt, Shirley Barker, Kevin Stone, John Brown & Andrew White

Left: The Highland Gathering, 1999 (presided over by Brell Ewart) who walks in front of the Mayor and his wife Angela in the parade along Compton

The Mayor at the opening of the library at St Oswald's School, October 1999

The Mayor, with James Spencer (left) and George Shaw (right), receiving a cheque for £150 towards the town's Millennium clock

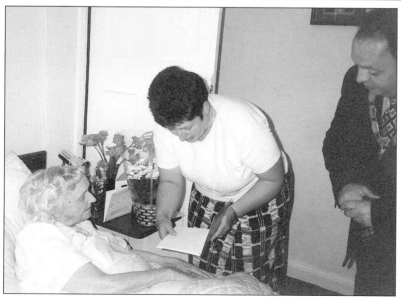

In May 2000, Ethel French celebrated her 100th birthday and the Mayor & Mayoress, Alan & Angela Hodkinson, called in to celebrate the event on behalf of the town

The Mayor of Ashbourne always plays a prominent part in the luncheon proceedings at Shrovetide. Here he is on each day with the turner-up – John Hanson on the Tuesday and Philip Tomlinson on the Wednesday of 2000. It was the first time that two members of the

Shrovetide Committee had turned up the ball in the same year for many years. John Hanson gave the longest speech ever (or at least in living memory) and the game was delayed on the Tuesday by the untimely death of an old and respected friend – Alec Robinson.

Above: The Mayor & Mayoress at the Ashbourne Lions Charter Anniversary dinner and dance, November 1999

Below: Fund raising for the new clock with (l-r): Alan Hodkinson; Andrew White (Mayor 2002-03); Andrew Birch and Mrs Pam Woodyatt

Unveiling of the new clock. The Mayor & Mayoress with Patrick McLoughlin MP left, and Lady Hilton (right)

Above: Guests and friends pose for a photograph at the unveiling

Below: The inauguration of the new Mayor in May 2000. Alan Hodkinson hands over his chain of office to Simon Spencer. The new Mayoress, Joanne Spencer, receives her chain from Angela Hodkinson

A sign on what is now "The Gingerbread Shop" (St John Street) proclaims: "God Save the King". Smith's Tavern was then Smith & Son. It shows rather well the building now demolished in the centre-right of the photograph

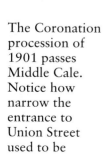

The Coronation procession of 1901 passes Middle Cale. Notice how narrow the entrance to Union Street used to be

A lovely photograph taken in Church Street, probably in 1901 or 1910

The proclamation of George V in 1910, by William Coxon, butcher and chairman of the
Council (and also the Shrovetide Committee). He is on the right of the two gentlemen
with papers in their hands

Above: Another gathering, perhaps for the Coronation of George V

Below: May Day in the Market Place. Notice the maypole (top left). The shops are Woodisse & Desborough, ironmongers and HP Hansen (? The shop of the photographer). The May Day parade was started by saddler Fred Sellars, who died in 1910

Above: This view of the proclamation of Edward VII shows the predecessors of Mr Hansen's shop, Lovatts who seem to have given their name to Lovatt's Yard

Below: The Coronation celebrations for George V included quite a large carnival, with a Carnival King and Queen, a procession and other festivities.

The views above, below and opposite, would appear to show the Carnival King & Queen. The view above may have been in the Park, with the trees lining Sandy Lane, now Park Road. The one below is on the Park, with Derby Road and the Stepping Fields in the distance

Above: An early 20th century procession outside The Corner House

Below: A Coronation procession (?1911) in Church Street. Note the sign for the Circulating Library on the rear building

Above: St John's Bible Class in 1908. Nearly all the ladies are clearly showing the then latest fashion in hair styling

Below: The 9th Duke of Devonshire campaigning during a General Election. It may well be November 1922, for he had been away since October 1916 as Governor-General of Canada. The scenes is in Compton

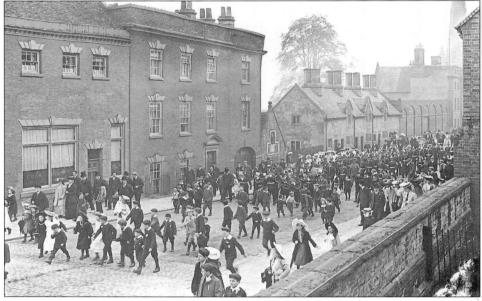

Top: A carnival procession proceeding along St John Street

Middle: A further procession in Church Street in Edwardian times

Bottom: Ashbourne Scouts leaving the Market Place. The postcard is dated May 1909

Further views of one of the town's early carnivals (this page & following page).
Unfortunately, none are dated

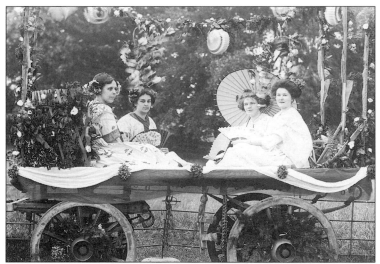

Another, more sombre scene in Station Road: The funeral of Police Supt Burford, who died in March, 1913. He founded the swimming club, sat on the Shrovetide Committee and established the town's Emergency & Relief Association (to help poor people in distress)

Above: Celebrations in Victoria Square

Below: Advertising the visit of Pastor Fletcher to preach on the subject "Is There A Hell?" at the Town Hall. This was taken in Station Road

Above: A gathering of local people, perhaps for a wedding (as it includes a vicar).
Unfortunatly the location cannot be indentified

Below: Olga Emery presenting a bouquet to General Booth upon leaving "The Ivies" in
Church Street: a postcard view by Mr Hansen

Above: A party to celebrate the end of the war for residents of Peter Street, Park Road and Sturston Road. It's taken in the garden of F P Birch on the corner of Park Road/ Sturston Road. The buildings behind are the Machine Inn and adjacent house (see p71)

Below: The Ashbourne Flying Club Dinner at The New Inns, near Alsop-en-le-Dale

Above: Staff of R Cooper & Co Ltd at the time of the Queen's Coronation, 1953

Below: Local residents celebrating the Queen's Coronation, 1953, at the hall situated near the end of Green Lane on Mayfield Road. It was close to where the bus stop now stands and has been demolished

The Offcote &
Underwood Corona-
tion celebrations,
1953. These were held
in a field just above
The Green Hall

Above: Another gathering on The Paddock of Station Street residents, celebrating the 1953 Coronation

Below: Bunting in nearby South Street for the Queen's Coronation

Above: Another view taken in Station Road. This is a photograph of a float in 1955 in the town's carnival

Below: A Scout jamboree in 1957 on The Paddock in Station Road. In the background is the Railway Station and the Station Hotel (now Beresford Arms Hotel)

The Rotary Club began in Ashbourne in November, 1946, with an initial six members: Robert Rose, George Gather, Charles Aitken, Michael Sadler, Frank Parry and William Spencer. Here are some early views of the club's Ladies Evenings etc.

Above: 1948, back (l-r): Robert Rose, George Gather, Frank Bromwich, Michael Sadler (President), Randall Pearson, Veronica Rose, Ellis Grimshaw, Kathleen Gather.
Front: (l-r) Bobby Sadler, Hilda Bromwich, Gladys Grimshaw, Florence Pearson

Conference photograph, 1958, (l-r): Dorothy Callow, Beryl Rose, Elsie Moore, George Rose, Ellis Grimshaw, Norman Moore, Roger Wright (President), Barbara Wright, Hector Callow

Above: 1966, (l-r): Elsie & Norman Reese, Jane Dawson, Ellis Grimshaw, Jessie & Arthur Parry (President), May Archer, Denis & Agnes Moore, John Archer, Frank O'Dowd

Below: 1984, Back (l-r): Harold Salt, Alan Smith, Clive Chipchase, Ken Bayliss (President). Front (l-r): Jane Smith, Margery Salt, Janet Bayliss, Rachel Chipchase

Above: The Rotary Ladies Evening at the Green Man Hotel, 1955 (l-r): Ellis Grimshaw, Gladys Grimshaw, Judith Sellors, Muriel Gammage, John Sellors, Janet Bayliss

Below: The Rotary Club Ball, Town Hall, January 1952

Above: Dawson, Macdonald & Dawson's works dinner. Back row (l-r): Eric Burford, Roy Bennett, Ted Rich, Ron Burford, Eric Redfern, Joe Bull, Edward Mee. Front row (l-r): Jill Challinor, ?, Mrs Bowler, Daphne Bennett, Mrs Jessie Burford, Mrs Maureen Rich and Mrs Grace Burford

Below: The Wakebourne Band, a regular feature in the town's carnival, seen in c. 1950. The lad at the front is Peter Blood

Staff of Sheila Spencer's shop off on a trip to a textile mill in West Yorkshire.
(Sheila can be seen at the front)

A gig at The George & Dragon with the Georgettes in 1962, starring Georgina Startin and ? Frank Higton (right)

Above: Part of the celebrations for the Silver Jubilee

Right: A fancy dress party at St John's House, St John Street, then the home of the Rose's

Above: Ashbourne Ladies Circle Coffee Morning, Town Hall, 1979, (l-r): Terry Brookes, Janet Bayliss, Gladys Bussell, Ann Manderville, Val Smith, Margaret Whyte

Below: The Clifton Ex-Servicemen's Dinner, 1977, (l-r): Rev Fred Ross, ?, Roger Harris, Jim Harrison, Jim Gourley, Gordon Green, Ellis Grimshaw, John Gammage

Above: In 1984 Mrs Sandra Lewer became Ladies Circle Area Chairman for Derbyshire and Nottinghamshire and a celebration was held at Cassandra's. Among those pictured are: Jennifer Dawson, Frances Gould, Margaret Dawson, Val Kirtley, Terry Brooks, Jean Forsyth, Francoise Mordey, Ann MacDarmaid, Irene Wilson, Viv Thomson, Sandra Lewer, Yvonne Towl and Gwen Davison

Below: In honour of Mrs Lewer's Lancashire origins, members of Ashbourne Round Table made an unscheduled visit to the celebration to serenade the assembled ladies with songs of old Lancashire in Eric Morecambe style flat caps and macs. Pictured (l to r): Paul Kirtley, Allen Forsyth, Colin Wilson, Graham Ashurst, Richard Swabey, Phillip Hunt, Danny Towl, Keith Foster, Frank Gould, Phil Brooks, Ian MacDarmaid (obscured), Johnny Dawson, Eddie Leyland, Mike Hyde, John Bailey and Bryan Davison

Above: Attending a Civic Reception in Ashbourne Town Hall in 1990 are the town's Scouts, Guides, Rangers and Ventures and their guests from Japan, Scotland and Sweden who were attending Peak 90, an international Scout and Guide camp held every 5 years at Chatsworth. Among those pictured are: Cllr Jack Moore, Cllr George Ward, Cllr Colin Clayton, Cllr Bertie Birch, Cllr Ian Bates, Cllr Fred Elliot, Sandra Lewer, Irene Blackshaw, Rose Dias, Barry Dias, Rachael Lewer, Andrew Wilson, Robert Wilson, Janet Adin, Polly Day, Karen Matthews, Elizabeth Hall, Mrs Hirae, Mrs Yamaguchi & Akio Yamada

Right: Ashbourne Tangent dedicated a bench for the town's Heritage Trail on 6th August 1996. Cutting the ribbon is Kay Orme, toasted by (l to r): Rosie Butt, Judith Sadler, Barbara Lowe, Sally Wall, Ann Mandeville, Elaine Hopkin & Alison Wright.

Models posing with the latest fashions around town for Sheila Spencer.
Sheila held many successful fashion shows at the Town Hall, Green Man
and at the Empire Ballroom. They were taken c. 1960

A Few Sporting Occasions

Ashbourne Football Club players pose for a photograph. It was taken prior to 1920, as Joe Burton retired from playing association football in 1919

Back row: (l-r): (?), Trevor Gerrard, Wm Prince, W Allsopp, J Haycock, Rev Hazelhurst, - Burton, ?, - Etherington

Middle row: C Bell, W Lee, B Walker, W Midlane

Front row: Joe Burton, G Dakin, F Jones, A Moreton, G Ainsworth

It appears to have been taken outside Ashbourne Hall Hotel, where Wm Prince was the proprietor from 1900-1910, so it may date from that period. Regrettably, the history of the town's football and cricket clubs (including the long-established Clifton Cricket Club) have not been written. In fact none of its sporting activities have been collated, with the obvious exception of the Shrovetide Football game.

Opposite page; Above: The crowd spills into Shaw Croft between the River Henmore (at Compton Bridge) and The Terrace, on the left (now the site of the Health Centre). Probably taken at Shrovetide, but Shaw Croft was also used for other events. At one time it had a running track and football pitch

Below: Shrovetide 1909 outside the old Coach & Horses pub in Dig Street. Behind is the Langley House school, which was run by Miss Sutton and had its playgound on the roof

ASHBOURNE AMATEUR BOXING CLUB
(Affiliated D.A,B.A,)

Grand BOXING TOURNAMENT

In the ASHBOURNE TOWN HALL·
Saturday, Oct. 30th, 1948   Comm. 7-0 p.m.

**Prizes to be presented by Mr. Stephen D. Player
Ednaston Manor**

PROGRAMME

BLUE   PRICE 3d.   RED

Contests not necessarily in Order of Appearance

Lt. Heavy Contest—Six 2 minute Rounds

✓ J. MARSH   v.   D. LOWNDES
Alfreton ABC.   Ashbourne ABC.

Welter Weight Contest—Six 2 minute Rounds

C. BIRD   v.   GUY HARRISON ✓
Raleigh AC.   Ashbourne ABC.
Notts. ABA. Welter Champion 1947—48

Light Weight Contest—Six 2 minute Rounds

✓ K. WINFIELD   v.   A MITCHELL
Raleigh AC. NEWBURY   Ashbourne ABC.

Welter Weight Contest—Four 3 minute Rounds

J. GUYATT   v   F. HOLLINSHEAD ✓
Raleigh AC.   Ashbourne ABC.

Feather Weight Contest—Six 2 minute Rounds,

E. CARTER   v.   J. BAILEY.   ✓
Raleigh AC.   MANN   Ashbourne and Spa ABC.
Notts. ABA. Champion, 1947—48

Junior Contest—Three 1½ minute Rounds

K. JOHNSON   v.   A MOORE   ✓
Alfreton ABC.   Ashbourne and Spa ABC's.

Light Weight Contest—Four 2 minute Rounds

✓ L. DALEY   v.   W. GODDARD
Raleigh AC.   Ashbourne ABC.

Bantam Weight Contest—Four 2 minute Rounds

✓ D. FEATHERSTONE v.   L. RENSHAW
Raleigh AC.   Ashbourne ABC.

Middle Weight Contest—Six 2 minute Rounds

D. LAMB ✓   v.   G. REYNOLDS
Raleigh AC.   Alfreton ABC.

Junior Contest—Three 1½ minute Rounds

✓ W. ARCHER   v.   R. BONSOR
Raleigh AC.   Ashbourne and Spa ABC's.

M.C.—J. W. TUNNICLIFFE   M.O.—Dr. J. HOLLICK
Referee, Judges and Timekeeper—Derby ABA. Officials
Hon. Sec.—E. T. W. LEIGH   Tournament Sec.—S. L. HILL
Hon. Treas.—R T MASON   Trainer—J. HOUSE

The programme for a 1948 Boxing Tournament held at Ashbourne Town Hall. The rear of the programme carried adverts for Massey & Jennings, shoe shop/repairers of the Market Place; Hill & Mainwaring, decorators of Buxton Road; and J M Winfield, trading as C Hales, printers. Presumably the ticks mark the winners of each contest

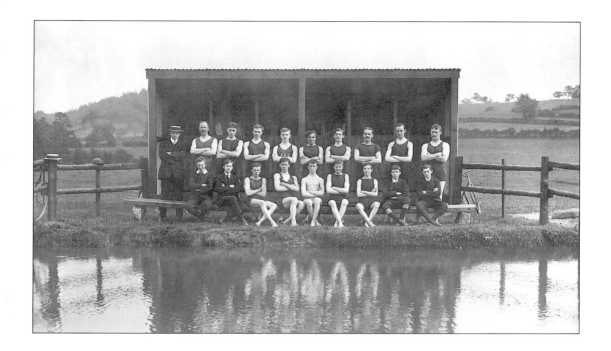

Above: The Ashbourne Bathing Club in 1912. Its "swimming pool" was the River Henmore, downstream from Sturston Mill, established by Supt Burford in July 1908 (see p. 135). Only male bathers were allowed to become members

Below: This photograph is not dated, but is presumably of the same era

Above: Club members taking a dip in the river

Below: The Ashbourne & District Schools Football League Cup Winners of 1939

Above: The Mappleton football team at Hinchley Wood

Below: The Nestlé tug of war team of 1919

Above: Sports Day on Shaw Croft 1906. The spectators are sitting with their backs to the river

Below: One of the Ashbourne football teams between the Wars. Only two names are known: J W Walker (standing first left) and Fred Ward (second from left on the front row)

Two snap shots of the St John's Cricket team in the 1920s-30s. Above: Back row (l-r): Wm Walker, Harry Stanley, Norman Middleton. Seated (l-r): Mr Rich, Joe Hambleton, Harold Wetton, Norman Smith, Tom Hambleton. Front: Ted Rich.

Below: Back: Harold Slater. Standing, (l-r): Tom Hambleton, Harry Stanley, William Walker, Les Watson. Seated, (l-r): ? Mr Rich, Ernest Sallis, Fred Hambleton, Joe Hambleton. Front: Ted Rich

Above: A motor cycle race in the Ashbourne area, taken by Mr Hansen

Below: A comic cricket match on Shaw Croft, from a postcard of 1917

Above: Opening of the Grammar School pavilion on the recreation ground with (l-r:) (?) The Duchess of Devonshire, The Duke of Devonshire, G M Bond, Miss Mary Bond & Major Weston Bond

Below: The opening of the Recreation Ground pavilion in 1957 (l-r:) George Gather, Sir Ian Walker & Joseph Lowe

Above: The new bandstand in the Memorial Grounds being formally opened in 1952

Below: An early bowls match

Right: Ashbourne Tennis Club in 1947/48, when they played Sheffield at Ashbourne. Left-right: D Shivers (Sheffield), R A Hibbins (Sheffield), D Daft, D Walker, A Keyworth (Sheffield) and D Sellers. R A Hibbins was a founder member of the Ashbourne Club in 1934-55, which survived for twenty years until season 1954-1955

Left: 1949-50 Derbyshire TT Championship. Winners of the Men's Singles, Men's Doubles and Mixed Doubles: D Sellers, D Simms and D Walker

Right: The club in the 1949-50 season at its annual dinner at the Peveril of the Peak Hotel. On the front row are (l-r): D Sellers, D Walker, G Senson (Chairman), R Rose (President) and D Daft, (?). During this season the club won the following: Derbyshire League Championship; The Derbyshire – Challenge Cup, Men's Singles; Men's Doubles; Mixed Doubles; The Staffordshire Men's Singles; The North Staffordshire Men's singles: The Derby Men's Singles; The Ashbourne & District League. It was a very creditable performance

PNEU School Nativity Play 1971. (Pictured are:) Caroline Oakden, Jill Bostock, Fiona Robinson, Sally Dauce, Cherry Douglas-Jones, Helen Rowley, Stephanie Bury, Claire Bury, Susan Berrisford, Rebecca Chambers, Jill Adams, Hazel Ducker, Henrietta Stevenson, Fiona Stevenson, Caroline Bownier, Barbara Strachan, Catherine Pearson, Camilla Brindley, Catrina Strachan, Sarah Merrington, Sarah Jones, Susan Smith & Sara Bayliss

Below: Rev. Lisemore & Irene Blackshaw. 1st Ashbourne Brownies with the presentation of a bench to St Oswalds Church

Above: This looks like one of the church schools gathered together for a photograph of a play

Below: The Church of England Infants School Christmas Concert in 1927

C.E.Infants
School,
Ashbourne.
"Concert"
Xmas.1924.

Above: This is possibly the girls class at the National School, but even the date is unknown

Below: Ashbourne Primitive Methodist Sunday School Treat, 1906

Above: Here is a scene of the early days on the Green Road site of the Grammar School with the laying of the foundation stone, 23 September, 1907

Below: Staff and guests at the Grammar School Fair, February 26, 1930

The newly completed school from the playing field and a more dramatic aerial view

Above: The original assembly room, now the library

Below: Empire Day at the Wesleyan School, 1933.
Back row; (l-r): Bill Hellaby, Dennis Burton, Jack Woodyatt, Jack Skinner, Clark Fowler. 2nd row Standing, (l-r): Eileen Salisbury, Gladys Thornley, Chrisitine Milland, Joan Radford, Don Dawson, Sam Stubbs, Frank Tomlinson, Dennis Handley. Front row, (l-r): Dorothy Fowler, Madge Hutchinson, Dennis Walker, Don Dudley

Above: The Upper Sixth of QEGS pictured on the steps of the Green Road site in May 1989, just prior to their A level examinations. Pictured are (l to r): Neil Parker, Robert Ware, Catherine Addison, Glen Redfern (obscured), Melanie Glendenning, Gail Mitchell, Helen Johnstone, Chris Saunders, Ben Davis, Kerry Brown, Lucy Miller, Hedi Ford (Head Girl), Bruce Drew (Head Boy), Matthew Morley, Naomi Dawson, John Archer, Robert Brown, Rebecca Turner, David Bowles, David Jones, Alex Tomlinson, Sue Crawley, Steve Alton, Diane Hogbin, Robert Wilson, Sue Coote, Darren Jennings, Ann Mainwaring, Andrew Wilson, Andrew Lewer, Michael Richardson (obscured), Johnny Bates, David Rose, John Chater, Richard Lewis, Alan Wheatley (teacher)

Below: QEGS sixth formers formed the company 'Jet Comb' which won both the Derbyshire and East Midlands regional finals of the 2002 Young Enterprise scheme. They then went forward to the national finals, held at the Ritz, London, and won third prize. Here they are pictured after their victory at the Derbyshire finals, held in Chesterfield. Pictured are (l to r): Fiona Bailey, Charles DeNobrga, Caroline Milne, Laura Evans, Ian Mainwaring, Nicola Oliver, Chris Jordan, William Bartholomew

Above: In 1997, extensive work was carried out on Ashbourne Methodist Church, reversing years of accumulated structural and cosmetic deterioration. Here we see the green container provided to Bentley's shop while their premises were repaired, doubtless full of sweet jars, boxes of coffee and tea and other vital provisions

Left: As part of the renovations the Methodist Church converted the former driving test centre into The Cornerstone, a tea shop which the Church also uses as function rooms

Above: Project 2000 was the name given to the programme of restoration, which involved a major fund-raising drive by Church members. Here the large scale of the brick repointing work can be seen

Below: The majority of the Church restoration was undertaken internally and builders erected scaffolding to quite dizzying heights to paint and plaster the ceiling

New state of the art lighting and sound systems were subtly incorporated into re-painting, plastering and structural work, respecting the building's listed status but also improving its versatility. Indeed, since restoration, the Methodist Church has been used not only for services, weddings and funerals but for external functions, such as Queen Elizabeth's Grammar School Speech Days and the Rotary Club's Young Musician competitions

The River Dove showing Alrewas House (right) and the gable end of the terrace of mill cottages by the river, seen here in a worrying condition for the householders affected

The National United Order of Free Gardeners (a Friendly Society) crossing Hanging Bridge, 1908

Above: The Grange, along Birdsgrove Lane and now demolished, although a wall still stands. A Monkey Puzzle tree stood in front of the farm house and may be seen. It was demolished in the late 50s/early 60s

Below: This postcard dates from c.1924 and shows the former cheese factory. The sign reads "Edmund Buxton Builder" and presumably these were his premises. The coach was new and being delivered to the North Western Bus Co. The bus registration would appear to be DB5020

Hanging Bridge being widened. The view below shows the medieval bridge,
which still survives with a new addition on each side.
Notice the Rock Cottages, now demolished, above the left arch

Above: Work on the new bridge (see p. 177) must have caused considerable disruption to traffic, let alone the two pubs situated either side of it. Until licensing laws were harmonised a few years ago, the Queens Arms shut at 10.30pm and the Royal Oak at 11.00pm, causing a farcical 10.40pm rush across the bridge! Notice the narrowness of the old bridge

Below: Old Hall Farm, Middle Mayfield

OSMASTON

Osmaston has one of
the finest neo-Gothic
churches in the
county, built in
1845. In July 2002
it celebrated its
refurbishment after
a major restoration
scheme. Here are
two views of it in
Edwardian times.
It is well worth a
visit

Above: The village, looking towards the pub from the adjacent houses

Below: The village pond. It looks larger here and the trees have now gone

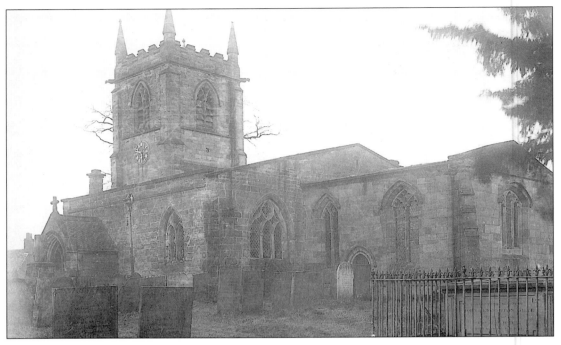

The vicar of Osmaston (see previous page) is currently the vicar of Shirley & Brailsford parishes (shown here in former times), together with Edlaston (not shown)

Above: St Michael's Church, Shirley   Below: All Saints, Brailsford

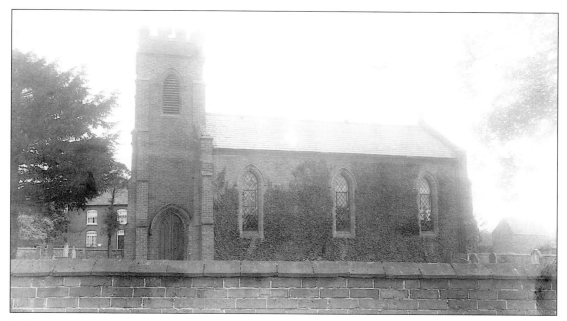

Above: Holy Trinity
Church, Yeaveley

Left: The dressing of
the Wyaston well

The lychgate at Clifton Church (above), with a similar design used on the entrance gate to the village cemetery

Above: The opening of the Lychgate, Clifton

Below: Chapel Lane, Clifton, showing what was the Sudbury Road. The fields have now been developed. The children are Ellis Grimshaw and his sister Mabel Ivy

The old Clifton signalbox seen insitu above, now at Consall Station
in the Churnet Valley (2002)

Above: The Queen Adelaide, Snelston. This old pub was full of character, customers taking their drinks in what amounted to the front room of the farm house. This photograph shows the farm just after the pub closed in 2000, but before it was significantly altered and converted into a private home

Left: Mr Cliff Lewer, Chairman of Snelston Parish Meeting and Councillor Mrs J Bevan, Chairman of Derbyshire Dales District Council, planting the Millennium Tree in the village in 2000

The big storm of 1962 left a trail of damage across the Peak District, from Sheffield to Ashbourne and Leek. The road from Clifton to Snelston used to be lined with trees planted by the Snelston estate, probably at the beginning of the 20th century. Alas three dozen of these fell victim to the storm and these views show the damage in Sprinkswood Lane and Snelston village. A large cedar tree fell across a house in Osmaston and about 90 of the trees on the drive of Osmaston Manor were also felled by the storm (see opposite, below)

Above: Snelston Village

Below: The Osmaston Manor drive used to have two twin rows of trees prior to the storm

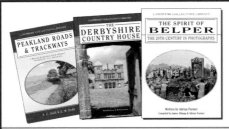

LANDM▲RK
COLLECTOR'S LIBRARY

LANDM▲RK
Publishing Ltd ● ● ●

Ashbourne Hall, Cokayne Ave, Ashbourne, Derbyshire, DE6 1EJ England☐
Tel 01335 347349 Fax 01335 347303 ☐
e-mail landmark@clara.net web site: www.landmarkpublishing.co.uk

Mining Histories
- Collieries of South Wales: Vol 1   *ISBN: 1 84306 015 9, £22.50*
- Collieries of South Wales: Vol 2   *ISBN: 1 84306 017 5, £19.95*
- Collieries of Somerset & Bristol   *ISBN: 1 84306 029 9, £14.95*
- Copper & Lead Mines around the Manifold Valley, North Staffordshire   *ISBN: 1 901522 77 6, £19.95*
- Images of Cornish Tin   *ISBN: 1 84306 020 5, £29.95*
- Lathkill Dale, Derbyshire, its Mines and Miners   *ISBN: 1 901522 80 6, £8.00*
- Rocks & Scenery the Peak District   *ISBN: 1 84306 026 4, paperback, £7.95*

Industrial Histories
- Alldays and Onions   *ISBN: 1 84306 047 7, £24.95*
- The Life & Inventions of Richard Roberts, 1789 -1864   *ISBN: 1 84306 027 2, £29.95*
- The Textile Mill Engine   *ISBN: 1 901522 43 1, paperback, £22.50*
- Watt, James, His Life in Scotland, 1736-74   *ISBN 1 84306 045 0, £29.95*
- Wolseley, The Real, Adderley Park Works, 1901-1926   *ISBN 1 84306 052 3, £19.95*

Roads & Transportantion
- Packmen, Carriers & Packhorse Roads   *ISBN: 1 84306 016 7, £19.95*
- Roads & Trackways of Wales   *ISBN: 1 84306 019 1, £22.50*
- Welsh Cattle Drovers   *ISBN: 1 84306 021 3, £22.50*
- Peakland Roads & Trackways   *ISBN: 1 901522 91 1, £19.95*

Regional/Local Histories
- Derbyshire Country Houses: Vol 1   *ISBN: 1 84306 007 8, £19.95*
- Derbyshire Country Houses: Vol 2   *ISBN: 1 84306 041 8, £19.95*
- Lost Houses of Derbyshire   *ISBN: 1 84306 064 7, £19.95, October 02*
- Well Dressing   *ISBN: 1 84306 042 6, Full colour, £19.95*
- Crosses of the Peak District   *ISBN 1 84306 044 2, £14.95*
- Shrovetide Football and the Ashbourne Game   *ISBN: 1 84306 063 9, £19.95*
- Historic Hallamshire   *ISBN: 1 84306 049 3, £19.95*
- Colwyn Bay, Its History across the Years   *ISBN: 1 84306 014 0, £24.95*
- Llandudno: Queen of Welsh Resorts   *ISBN 1 84306 048 5, £15.95*
- Llanrwst: the History of a Market Town   *ISBN 1 84306 070 1, £14.95*
- Lost Houses in and around Wrexham   *ISBN 1 84306 057 4, £16.95*
- Shipwrecks of North Wales   *ISBN: 1 84306 005 1, £19.95*